Illegal Animal Traffickers

D0912537

NEL YOMTOV

Children's Press®
An Imprint of Scholastic Inc.

Content Consultant
Albert E. Scherr, JD
Chair, International Criminal Law and Justice Programs
University of New Hampshire School of Law
Concord, New Hampshire

Library of Congress Cataloging-in-Publication Data
Yomtov, Nel.
 Illegal animal traffickers / by Nel Yomtov.
   pages cm. — (A true book)
 Includes bibliographical references and index.
 ISBN 978-0-531-21464-0 (library binding) — ISBN 978-0-531-22077-1 (pbk.)
 1. Wildlife smuggling—Juvenile literature. 2. Wildlife crimes—Juvenile literature. I. Title.
 HV6410.Y66 2016
 364.1'3367—dc23   2015023857

© 2016 Scholastic Inc.
All rights reserved. Published in 2016 by Children's Press, an imprint of Scholastic Inc. Published simultaneously in Canada. Printed in China 62
SCHOLASTIC, CHILDREN'S PRESS, A TRUE BOOK™, and associated logos are trademarks and/or registered trademarks of Scholastic Inc.
2 3 4 5 6 7 8 9 10 R 25 24 23 22 21 20 19 18 17 16

Front cover: A smuggled orangutan from Indonesia

Back cover: Snakes seized by park rangers in New Mexico

Find the Truth!

Everything you are about to read is true *except* for one of the sentences on this page.

Which one is **TRUE**?

T or F   Wildlife trafficking involves only animals that are sold as pets.

T or F   Illegal animal trafficking occurs on every continent.

Find the answers in this book.

3

Contents

THE **BIG** TRUTH!

The World's Most Trafficked Mammal

Pangolin

Illegally captured animals are often transported in containers that are too small for them.

African elephant

Oncillas are among the most common mammals to be trafficked from Central America.

CHAPTER 1

The Illegal Wildlife Trade

In September 2014, a German tourist waited at an airport in Costa Rica for his flight home. When security officers noticed him constantly adjusting his bag, they searched his luggage. Inside were 184 frogs, 42 lizards, 9 snakes, and 203 tadpoles stuffed into plastic containers. Many of the animals had died before authorities found them. The man was trying to **smuggle** the creatures out of the country. He is just one of tens of thousands of illegal animal traffickers in the world today. Some of them are caught. Unfortunately, many others are not.

What Is an Animal Trafficker?

Products such as meat, fur, and leather all come from animals. Most of the time, these products come from legal sources. Sometimes, however, they come from illegal sources. In these cases, the product comes from an animal **species** that is protected by laws to keep it from becoming **endangered** or even **extinct**. These laws often limit how a species can be hunted or if it can be hunted at all. Other laws control whether certain species can be brought in or out of a country.

Hunting some wild animals, such as kangaroos in Australia, is legal.

Smugglers may transport live animals in water bottles or similar containers.

Animal traffickers kill or capture protected animals and transport them illegally to supply a large worldwide trade. The illegal animal trade involves many people. **Poachers** hunt or trap protected animals. A series of people smuggle live animals and animal products past authorities through their own countries or into other countries. Finally, customers all around the world purchase the illegal items.

This market stall in Peru sells illegal Boa constrictor (*boa*) and turtle (*tortuga*) oils.

Rare Ingredients

Much of the illegal wildlife trade is fueled by the demand for products made from animals. Rhinoceros horns, elephant tusks, turtle shells, bear claws, fur from big cats, flesh from a range of species, and reptile skins are used to make everything from clothing to medicine. Some customers might want a coat made from tiger's fur. Others might want to taste the meat of an endangered animal or display its skull as a trophy.

The Pet Trade

The illegal wildlife trade also supplies the **exotic** pet market. Parrots, reptiles, and insects are among the most commonly captured animals. They are sold to private collectors, zoos, and museums. Even big cats may be sold as pets. Authorities estimate more tigers are kept as pets in the United States than live in the wild in Asia. Many of these animals suffer in **captivity** or damage the environment if they get loose.

Exotic or unusual animals such as cuscus, a type of marsupial related to kangaroos and koalas, are popular pets in many places around the world.

Why Is Wildlife Trafficking Thriving?

Most traffickers get into the illegal animal trade because it is very profitable. The businesspeople who arrange the capture, smuggling, and sale of wildlife can make enormous sums of money. Also, in some parts of the world, animal trafficking is considered a minor crime. Many law enforcement organizations do not have enough resources to enforce laws against poaching and trafficking.

An antipoaching team patrols the Lewa Wildlife Conservancy in Kenya.

As many as 40 Siberian tigers are illegally killed each year in Russia.

A Low-Risk Business

Animal traffickers rarely have to fear getting caught. Most wilderness areas where they kill or capture animals are vast. The law enforcement officials patrolling these areas are unable to monitor all trafficking activities. Even when traffickers are caught, the punishments they receive are usually not severe. In many cases, the stolen wildlife is merely taken away or a small fine must be paid.

A market stall sells illegal turtle shells and seashells in Madagascar.

CHAPTER 2

Worldwide Criminals

With such a large amount of money to make and a low risk of getting caught, the illegal animal trade draws in many people. Organized crime groups, large companies, international terrorists, and **indigenous** peoples are among those involved in this type of crime. Most animal trafficking operations involve people from these different groups working together.

Turtle species in Madagascar are among the rarest in the world.

Tiger skins can cost thousands of dollars each.

Organized Crime

Wildlife trafficking operations are usually planned very well. Organized crime groups hire, equip, and supervise a number of employees to help them obtain and distribute illegal wildlife. Poachers on the ground find the animals, while workers called agents move them around the country. People called exporters smuggle the animals across international borders. Sellers deliver them to customers willing to pay the highest price.

Paid to Capture and Kill

Organized crime groups, passing themselves off as legal businesses, often pay indigenous peoples to hunt wildlife. In Malaysia, local people have hunted tigers to meet the Asian demand for body parts used in traditional medicine. In Brazil, farmers are paid to collect and trap animals from forests and other local **habitats**. In some cases, the income from animal trafficking is all people can rely on to survive.

Sellers and buyers haggle over a price for *yartsa gunbu* in Tibet. People must carry a license and pay a tax to legally gather these fungus-infected caterpillars.

The Role of Terrorists

Terrorist groups are also involved in the illegal wildlife trade. Al-Shabaab in Somalia gets up to 40 percent of its funding from the illegal ivory trade in Africa. Al-Shabaab members do not only kill rare animals. They have been accused of killing wildlife wardens who would have stopped the hunting, too. Other violent groups, such as the Lord's Resistance Army in Uganda and South Sudan, may operate on profits from animal trafficking as well.

Members of Al-Shabaab patrol the streets of Mogadishu, Somalia.

Cages at a market in Mong La, Myanmar, display badgers, rare birds, pangolins, and monkeys for sale.

Markets and Restaurants

Illegal wildlife markets and restaurants thrive in many **developing countries**. For some people in these places, hunting animals is an important part of their culture or religion. In the town of Mong La in Myanmar, along the border with China, outdoor shops sell elephant hides and tusks, leopard and bear skins, antelope skulls, and other items. Sun bear meat and monkey meat are common dishes served in restaurants there.

The Golden Triangle Special Economic Zone is filled with fancy casinos, hotels, and restaurants.

A region known as the Golden Triangle Special Economic Zone is located in northern Laos. Though in Laos, this area is officially controlled by a Chinese company. The zone experiences little policing from Laos or China. Restaurants there serve food and drinks made with parts from tigers, Asiatic bears, pangolins, and other protected animals. Visitors to the area can also purchase illegal wildlife products such as ivory.

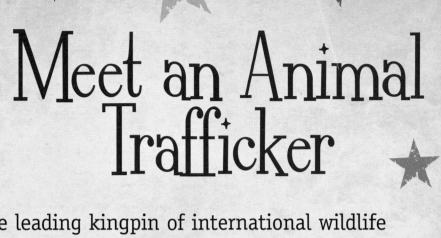

Meet an Animal Trafficker

The leading kingpin of international wildlife smugglying may be Vixay Keosavang. He is especially notorious for smuggling rhinoceros horns and elephant tusks. Vixay also keeps dozens of living tigers, bears, lizards, and other creatures in his compound in Laos. Investigators think Vixay's empire stretches from wild habitats in Africa and Asia to wealthy buyers in China and Vietnam. According to some experts, however, Vixay's connections within the Laotian government prevent him from being caught.

A scientist in Peru holds a baby giant anteater that was rescued from smugglers.

CHAPTER 3

Wildlife Trafficking Hot Spots

Animal trafficking occurs on every continent. Hot spot regions where traffickers both capture and sell illegal wildlife include China's borders, eastern and southern Africa, Southeast Asia, and Eastern Europe. The Caribbean and South Pacific are also important providers and purchasers of trafficked goods. The United States is one of the world's major destinations for illegally trafficked wildlife, second only to China.

Peru's many species of wildlife are prized by animal collectors.

A Global Problem

A great deal of trafficking takes place in Asia. Parrots, tortoises, freshwater turtles, snakes, and lizards are captured as pets for worldwide distribution. Tibetan antelope are killed for their wool, which is woven into shawls worth up to $15,000 in Western nations. In Russia, eggs are cut from protected fish called sturgeon and sold as food. In China, Siamese crocodiles, shark fins, and tiger meat are hunted and eaten as delicacies.

The Tibetan antelope is considered endangered, with a rapidly decreasing population.

Asia
parrots, pangolins, reptiles

North America
black bears, bighorn sheep, and white-tailed deer

Europe
bird eggs, predatory birds

Africa
elephants and rhinoceroses

Australia
snakes, lizards, birds

South America
rain forest animals, including birds, monkeys and other mammals, reptiles, and insects

This map lists major sources of illegally trafficked wildlife in every continent except Antarctica.

In Africa, elephant ivory and rhino horns are the most widely hunted and trafficked illegal animal parts. In South America, a huge range of rain forest animals is illegally sold as pets and food. Skins are also made into purses, boots, and belts. In North America, some hunters kill the black bear for its paws, which they use to make bear paw soup. Other people want to display antlers as trophies, so they hunt bighorn sheep and white-tailed deer.

The World's Most Trafficked Mammal

The gentle pangolin is a small insect-eating creature that lives mainly in the jungles of Asia. It is sometimes a source of meat for local people. It is also the world's most heavily trafficked mammal species. The pangolin is the only mammal completely covered in scales. This is what makes it coveted prey for traffickers.

The pangolin's scales are believed to have medicinal value, especially in China. In this country, dried scales are cooked and eaten by people who hope to cure a variety of conditions. Such illnesses include nervousness, deafness, and malaria.

When in danger, a pangolin rolls into a ball to protect itself. This allows smugglers to bundle the animals into a sack for easy carrying. At about 10 to 60 pounds (5 to 27 kg) each, a trafficker can reasonably carry more than one pangolin at a time. It is

believed that more than 10,000 pangolins are trafficked each year. Six of the world's eight pangolin species are endangered or threatened. As the pangolin population dwindles in Asia, traffickers are turning to Africa, where the creature also lives. Experts fear that illegal trafficking could drive the pangolin to extinction very soon.

A customs agent in France checks a shipment of tortoises.

CHAPTER 4

The Ways of the Trafficker

Traffickers don't always seize wild animals from natural habitats. Sometimes they legally breed them in captivity. This helps them mask illegal activities. To smuggle animals out of a country, traffickers may breed 50 exotic birds a year but tell authorities they have bred 100. The additional 50 birds are illegally captured from the wild. Traffickers use a variety of tricky methods like this to sneak animals into different countries.

 Authorities seize tens of thousands of turtles and tortoises each year.

Authorities in Germany caught smugglers hiding live turtles in cigarette boxes.

Masters of Disguise

Another method of sneaking animals across international borders is to disguise them. Traffickers in New Guinea frequently remove the long, colorful feathers of birds of paradise and dye the birds black. The disguised birds are then included with legal shipments of crows or mynah birds to other countries. In 2013, officials in Macau seized 75 pounds (34 kilograms) of ivory covered in chocolate and hidden inside candy wrappers.

Hiding Places

To smuggle wildlife through airports, traffickers often hide animals in luggage, plastic containers, and secret compartments sewn into clothing. In 2002, a man at a California airport was arrested for smuggling two Asian leopards and several birds of paradise, all of them alive, in his luggage. When the man was searched, officials also found two living pygmy monkeys stuffed into his underwear.

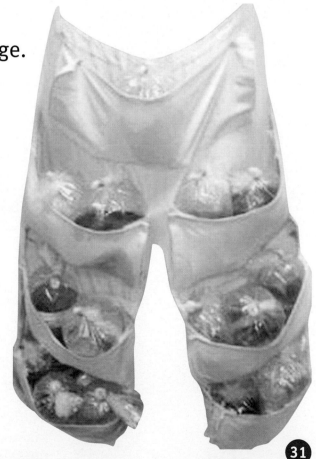

A woman in Australia hid live fish in plastic bags in these special pouches under her skirt.

A World Wide Web of Trafficking

In recent years, the Internet has become a major source for the trade of illegal pets and animal products. Traffickers also go online to buy equipment for their businesses. According to one smuggler, the Internet has caused an "explosion" in the illegal wildlife trade. With a few clicks, international collectors of exotic animals can easily purchase Bengal tigers, baby giraffes, rare flowers, and much more.

Animal Traffickers Timeline

1800
Roughly 26 million elephants live in Africa.

1900
The U.S. government passes the Lacey Act, banning the trade of wildlife that has been taken or transported illegally.

1975
The Convention on International Trade in Endangered Species of Wild Fauna and Flora (CITES) is created to protect wildlife around the world.

Internet traffickers often use secret code words to sneak past sites that monitor illegal trading on the Web. The term "four-wheeler" is used to indicate a star tortoise. "Striped T-shirt" stands for tiger skin. Abbreviations, such as "YTB" for yellow-tailed black cockatoo, are also commonly used. In 2014, the International Fund for Animal Welfare (IFAW) found that roughly 33,000 live wild animals were on sale online in 16 different countries in only the first few months of that year.

2015

Africa's elephant population falls to an estimated 470,000 to 600,000. More species become endangered or extinct each year.

1979

Only 1.3 million elephants remain in Africa.

Monkeys struggle for space in a box found in a smuggler's car trunk.

A Major Impact

Illegally trafficked animals are usually trapped and transported in cruel ways. Elephants and rhinos are usually shot. Their horns and tusks are cut away and their bodies left. Other types of animals, captured alive, are stuffed into small spaces such as plastic containers and luggage during long hours of transport. This causes pain, hunger, and stress. Many animals die before they reach their destination.

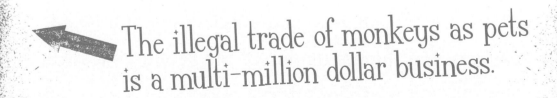

The illegal trade of monkeys as pets is a multi-million dollar business.

A tiger walks along a path in Ranthambore National Park in India.

Killing Off Earth's Wildlife

The illegal wildlife trade threatens many species. Hundreds are endangered, with many close to extinction. For example, about 3,000 tigers remain in the wild, down from the estimated 100,000 living at the beginning of the 20th century. More than half of the roughly 330 species of tortoises and freshwater turtles—traded mainly as food and pets—are considered threatened. Illegal trafficking has reduced the population of the scarlet macaw in Central America to less than 1,000.

Damage to the Environment

Obtaining wildlife illegally often harms the environment. Poachers frequently damage habitats, and removing too many animals from a location can leave other species with nothing to eat. In addition, trafficking introduces new species to a region. For example, Chinese mitten crabs are trafficked for food but sometimes escape into the wild. These animals compete with native species for food. Trafficking also spreads diseases carried by animals, threatening the health of humans and wildlife.

Burmese pythons have caused a lot of damage in Florida's wetlands after pet owners began releasing the exotic snakes into the wild.

Many places, including Tanzania, rely on money from tourists who come to see local animal species.

Effects on Local Communities

Trafficking takes necessary resources from poor people in nations where the activity takes place. It can also harm a community's tourism industry. Tourists may fear visiting places where dangerous criminals operate. A loss of tourism decreases the money earned by restaurants, hotels, and other businesses. In some parts of the world, these businesses are how people make most of their money. As a result, trafficking can ruin their way of life.

Animal Trafficking and World Health

Many diseases are transmitted from animals to humans. Outbreaks of Ebola have occurred because of human contact with monkeys, gorillas, chimpanzees, and bats. The disease is spread so easily that medical workers (below) must cover their entire bodies when working with patients. The origin of HIV is probably linked to humans eating wild meat. As wildlife trade continues, the chances of transmitting diseases between wildlife, humans, and domestic animals only increase.

Law enforcement arrested several fishers in the Philippines for illegally hunting sea turtles. Even when caught, most smugglers face only light penalties.

CHAPTER 6

A Difficult Battle

It is unlikely that illegal wildlife trafficking can be eliminated entirely. In recent years, however, many governments have increased their efforts to tackle this global menace. For example, Kenya has strengthened its wildlife protection laws and set harsher penalties for wildlife trafficking. China, a major destination for illegal wildlife products, has passed laws to reduce the amounts of rhino horn, elephant ivory, and shark fin purchased by its people.

All seven species of sea turtle are endangered.

A Worldwide Effort

Many nongovernmental organizations (NGOs) have joined the fight against animal trafficking. The Convention on International Trade in Endangered Species of Wild Fauna and Flora (CITES) is supported by more than 180 nations. It was created to protect animals and plants around the world. TRAFFIC, an NGO that monitors the wildlife trade, works with lawmakers, law enforcement authorities, and court systems to establish and enforce anti-trafficking laws worldwide.

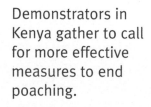

Demonstrators in Kenya gather to call for more effective measures to end poaching.

Park rangers at Kenya's Ol Pejeta Conservancy protect the few remaining northern white rhinos.

Rangers sometimes shorten a rhino's horns to discourage poachers.

You Can Make a Difference

There is a lot that individual people can do to help fight animal trafficking. Never buy illegal wildlife products or exotic animals. Support the efforts of **conservation** groups in the fight against animal trafficking. Most importantly, learn more about animal trafficking and what can be done to save Earth's precious wildlife. By sharing your knowledge, you can increase awareness of this global issue. ★

True Statistics

Value of illegal wildlife trade worldwide: $19 billion

Number of African elephants killed each day: 100

Number of pangolins traded illegally between 2000 and 2013: More than 1 million

Number of marine turtles illegally caught in Mexico between 2000 and 2014: 65,000

Number of animals stolen from Brazil's rain forest annually: 38 million

Price of one illegally stolen Lear's macaw: $60,000

Price of one illegal jaguar skin in the United States: $20,000

Number of tigers living in the wild worldwide: 3,000

Number of tigers kept as pets in the United States: 5,000

Did you find the truth?

F Wildlife trafficking involves only animals that are sold as pets.

T Illegal animal trafficking occurs on every continent.

Resources

Books

Baillie, Marilyn. *How to Save a Species*. Berkeley, CA: Owlkids, 2014.

Hirsch, Rebecca. *Helping Endangered Animals*. Ann Arbor, MI: Cherry Lake Publishing, 2010.

Jazynka, Kitson. *Mission Tiger Rescue: All About Tigers and How to Save Them*. Washington, DC: National Geographic, 2015.

Visit this Scholastic Web site for more information on illegal animal traffickers:
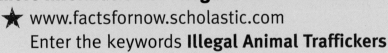 www.factsfornow.scholastic.com
Enter the keywords **Illegal Animal Traffickers**

Important Words

captivity (kap-TIV-i-tee) the condition of being held or trapped by people

conservation (kahn-sur-VAY-shuhn) the protection of wildlife, forests, and natural resources

developing countries (di-VEL-uhp-ing KUHN-treez) countries in which most people are poor and there is not yet much industry

endangered (en-DAYN-jurd) at risk of dying out completely

exotic (ig-ZAH-tik) from a faraway country

extinct (ik-STINGKT) no longer found alive

habitats (HAB-uh-tatz) the places where an animal or plant is usually found

indigenous (in-DIJ-uh-nuhs) originating in a particular region or country

poachers (POH-churz) people who hunt, fish, or gather plants illegally

smuggle (SMUHG-uhl) to move goods illegally in or out of a country

species (SPEE-sheez) one of the groups into which animals and plants of the same genus are divided

Index

Page numbers in **bold** indicate illustrations.

About the Author

Nel Yomtov is an award-winning author with a passion for writing nonfiction books for young readers. He has written books and graphic novels about history, geography, science, and other subjects. Nel has worked at Marvel Comics, where he edited, wrote, and colored hundreds of titles. He has also served as editorial director of a children's book publisher and as publisher of Hammond World Atlas books.

Yomtov lives in the New York City area with his wife, Nancy, a teacher. Their son, Jess, is a sports journalist.